Facing Mighty Fears
About Health

Dr. Dawn's Mini Books About Mighty Fears
By Dawn Huebner, PhD
Illustrated by Liza Stevens
Helping children ages 6–10 live happier lives

Facing Mighty Fears About Animals
ISBN 978 1 78775 946 6
eISBN 978 1 78775 947 3

Facing Mighty Fears About Throwing Up
ISBN 978 1 78775 925 1
eISBN 978 1 78775 926 8

Facing Mighty Fears About Trying New Things
ISBN 978 1 78775 950 3
eISBN 978 1 78775 951 0

Watch for future titles in the
Dr. Dawn's Mini Books About Mighty Fears series.

Facing Mighty Fears About Health

Dawn Huebner, PhD

Illustrated by Liza Stevens

Jessica Kingsley Publishers
London and Philadelphia

First published in Great Britain in 2022 by Jessica Kingsley Publishers
An imprint of Hodder & Stoughton Ltd
An Hachette Company

1

A CIP catalogue record for this title is available from the
British Library and the Library of Congress

ISBN 978 1 78775 928 2
eISBN 978 1 78775 927 5

Printed and bound in Great Britain by TJ Books Ltd

Jessica Kingsley Publishers' policy is to use papers that are natural,
renewable, and recyclable products and made from wood grown in
sustainable forests. The logging and manufacturing processes are expected
to conform to the environmental regulations of the country of origin.

Jessica Kingsley Publishers
Carmelite House
50 Victoria Embankment
London EC4Y 0DZ

www.jkp.com

Grown-ups:

Need ideas about how to use this book?

Please see Dr. Dawn's
Note to Parents and Caregivers
on page 67.

You'll also find a **Resource Section**
highlighting books, websites, and organizations
for parents of anxious kids.

Bodies!

When you stop to think about it, your body is a remarkable thing.

It can:

Swallow

BLINK

Ache

Bend

REACH

Wave

Lift

Scrunch down

Grow

Repair itself

Balance

Twist

Chew

Digest

Blow bubbles

Make noises

See

HEAR

Smell

Taste

AND SO MUCH MORE...

Even now, as you sit wherever you are sitting, your body is humming along, doing what it needs to do.

Your heart is **beating**, and your lungs are **expanding**, and your intestines are **digesting**.

Your senses are taking in information and so is your brain, which is thinking, and thinking, and thinking.

FUN FACT
Your ears and nose keep growing your whole life.

We often don't notice what our bodies are doing.

In fact, until you read the words "your heart is beating," you probably weren't aware of the lub-dub, lub-dub, lub-dub that is always, always there.

Why is that?

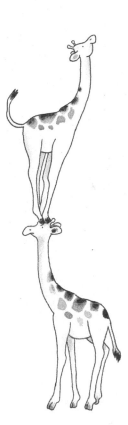

FUN FACT
The heart is one of the most powerful organs in the body, able to squirt blood 9 meters—almost 30 feet—into the air. That's as high as a giraffe with its neck extended balanced on the head of another giraffe, with its neck extended, too!

Why do we **not** notice our hearts beating and our lungs expanding and our intestines digesting?

And then, why do we suddenly start to notice these things, like maybe you are noticing them now?

Well, every moment of every day, our brains take in millions of bits of information.

We don't pay attention to all these bits—there are too many of them.

But when you read specific words, like "your heart is beating," your brain shifts your attention, and you begin to notice your own heart lub-dubbing along.

FUN FACT
The human heart beats 100,000 times a day, 36 million times a year, and over a billion times in 30 years. That's a lot of lub-dubs!

FUN FACT
Your circulatory system—the veins, arteries, and capillaries that move blood through your body—is over 60,000 miles (almost 97,000 kilometers) long. That's more than two times around the world.

For most people, that's a quick thing. You notice your heart—yup, there it is, **beating**—and then your attention shifts to other things.

But for some people, their attention doesn't shift. They notice something, and then they keep noticing it.

They become aware of their breathing, for example.

Or their swallowing.

And then they keep thinking about their breathing or their swallowing.

And they start to wonder, "Hey, is that working the way it's supposed to? Is everything okay in there?"

Perhaps that's what happens for you.

You notice something. And you keep noticing it. And then you start to wonder:

If you are a child who wonders about these sorts of things, you are not alone.

There are lots of children whose thoughts get stuck this way. Lots of children who think about and worry about their health.

Are they sick?

Are they going to get sick?

Is their body going to get a disease, or suddenly stop working?

FUN FACT
The average person thinks over 70,000 thoughts in a typical day.

Repeatedly thinking about and worrying about these things is called **Health Anxiety**, and it affects lots of kids.

Grown-ups, too.

Health Anxiety can make it hard to eat, sleep, go places, be with friends.

It can make it hard to pay attention, try new things, be by yourself, have fun.

Health Anxiety can get in the way, big time.

But here's the thing: you can learn about
Health Anxiety.

Get good at spotting it.

Start responding to it in a different way.

And once you do that, Health Anxiety won't have
the power to bother you anymore.

To understand about Health Anxiety, you need to know about the warning system in your brain.

We each have a small, almond-shaped part in our brain called the **amygdala** (a-mig-da-la). Actually, we have two, one on each side of the brain.

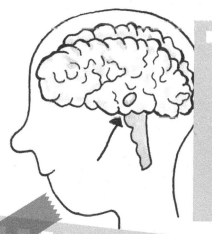

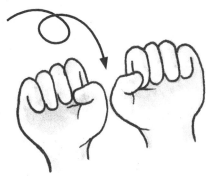

FUN FACT
The left side of your brain controls the right side of your body; the right side of your brain controls the left side of your body.

FUN FACT
If you hold your fists side-by-side, with your thumbs touching each other, that's just about the size of your brain.

The amygdala is a bit like a smoke detector, alerting us to possible danger.

But just like a smoke detector, it sometimes makes mistakes.

These are called **FALSE ALARMS**.

What is a false alarm?

FUN FACT
If all the iron in your body was gathered together, there would be enough to forge the screws needed to attach a smoke detector to your ceiling.

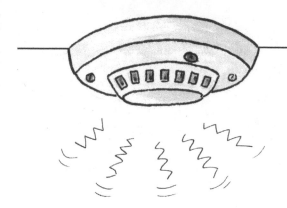

Well, in the case of a smoke detector, a false alarm is when the smoke detector **shrieks**, but there is no fire.

Has that ever happened in your house?

Has the smoke detector sounded its alarm even though there wasn't a fire?

Why did that happen?

FUN FACT
The average
human head has
100,000 hairs.

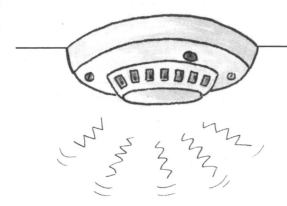

Well, smoke detectors sound their alarms when there is smoke. But smoke doesn't always mean fire.

Sometimes it means a candle is burning. Or meat is sizzling. Or toast is getting overdone.

A smoke detector can't tell the difference between smoke from a piece of overdone toast and smoke from a fire.

That's a problem, isn't it?

A fire is an emergency, but overdone toast is not. And yet, the smoke detector makes the same shrieking sound. The same alarm goes off every time.

Should you yank the smoke detector down from the ceiling and throw it away?

No, that wouldn't be the right thing to do. After all, you do need to know if there is a fire.

Should you panic every time the alarm shrieks, and immediately go racing out of your house?

No, that's not the right thing, either. It would be silly to run away from overdone toast.

What you need to do, instead, is understand how your smoke detector works.

Understanding the smoke detector makes it easier to spot false alarms.

It's the same with your brain alarm—
your amygdala.

You need to get to know it so when you start to feel scared, you can tell yourself, "Hey, that's my brain alarm."

And then you can figure out whether there's actual danger or not.

FUN FACT
Humans are the only animals that blush.

Imagine this:

It's a Saturday morning and you walk into the kitchen and see your dad making your favorite breakfast—pancakes.

Your amygdala remains quiet—there's no danger in pancakes! Instead, your brain **ZOOMS** in on the sights and sounds and smells that tell you a delicious treat is on the way.

FUN FACT
Between the surface of your tongue, the roof of your mouth, and your throat, you have close to 9,000 taste buds. No wonder pancakes taste so good.

But then you spot a syringe (also known as a shot)
on the counter, right next to your dad.

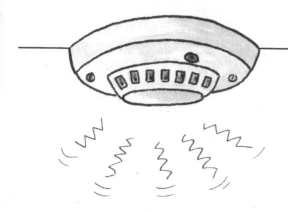

AMYGDALA ALERT!

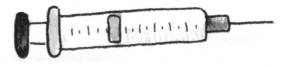

There goes your brain alarm!

Your eyes go wide, and your heart starts to **pound**.

You forget about the pancakes, and only
pay attention to the syringe.

Why is it there?!

Are you about to get a shot?!

Your dad explains that the shot is for your cat.

She needs to start taking special medicine for her diabetes—medicine that comes in a syringe.

Poor kitty.

But **phew!** The shot is not for you.

So, what will your brain shift back to?

(Hint: it's round and soft and sweet and yummy.)

FUN FACT
Just like everyone has their own fingerprints, we each have a unique tongue print, too.

Let's say the same thing happens the next morning.

You come down to waffles. Or breakfast burritos.
Or whatever else you love. And again, there's
that syringe.

The first few days, your amygdala might send out an ALERT, causing you to feel a jolt of fear…until you remember that the syringe has nothing to do with you.

And then after a while, you stop getting that amygdala ping.

Your brain has learned that the syringe isn't for you.

It's not important, so over time, your amygdala stops paying attention to it.

FUN FACT
Babies have more than 300 bones in their bodies. Grown-ups have only 206 bones. Do we lose bones as we get older?! Not really. What happens is that some of our bones fuse together, so two or three bones become just one.

Which brings us back to Health Anxiety.

Your brain has been noticing small things, normal things—like the way it feels to breathe or swallow or eat or move—and your amygdala is telling you, "Hey! Pay attention to this! Something might be wrong here!"

Or maybe, once, something did go wrong. Maybe a piece of food got stuck when you were swallowing.

Or you felt lightheaded when you were outside on a hot day.

Or maybe you found out that your grandfather had a heart attack, and your parents explained what that meant.

And suddenly, your amygdala is on HIGH ALERT about every little thing.

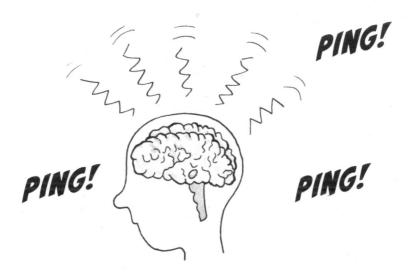

Before you started reading this book, you might not have known that your amygdala sometimes makes mistakes (false alarms, remember?), so maybe you believed your amygdala, every time.

That makes sense.

When your amygdala sets off an alarm, it sure seems as if something must be wrong.

So maybe you started to do things to protect yourself, like asking to have your temperature taken (to make sure you aren't sick).

Or eating only soft foods (so you don't choke).

Or insisting that your parents stay with you while you fall asleep (in case you stop breathing).

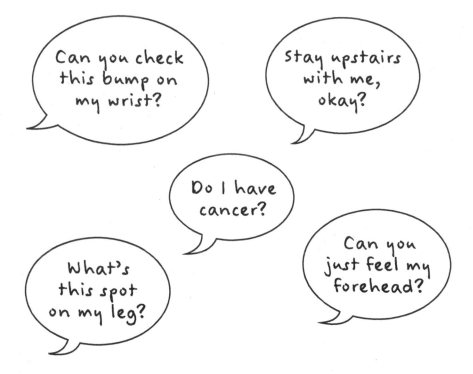

Chances are good that you've been doing these things to protect yourself because your amygdala has been telling you that something is wrong.

Trying to protect yourself every time you have a brain alarm helps you feel better, but it actually makes the problem worse.

FUN FACT
People shed their skin—just like snakes do—only not all at once. Human skin flakes off just a little bit at a time, and new skin grows in its place. If you live to be 80, you will have 1000 different skins.

Trying to protect yourself every time you have a brain alarm makes you think you **have to** protect yourself.

So, you do something to protect yourself.

And then you get caught in a loop of having a false alarm, believing it, and immediately doing something to keep yourself safe.

FALSE ALARM

TRY TO PROTECT
YOURSELF

BELIEVE IT

Except you weren't in danger to begin with. It was a false alarm.

It's like panicking and running out of the house immediately when your smoke detector shrieks, rather than taking a moment to look around, and seeing that all you have to do is pop the bread out of the toaster.

So, if you're a kid who worries about your health, if you've been asking lots of questions or changing your behavior because you are afraid that your body isn't working the way it's supposed to—or that something is about to go terribly wrong—here's what you need to do:

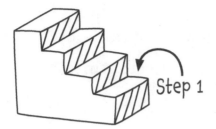

Step 1

1. Learn about your amygdala (brain alarm).

You've already started to learn about your amygdala, just by reading this book.

Re-read the book if you need to. Then remind yourself that your amygdala alerts you to things that **might** be dangerous, but there are LOTS of false alarms.

If your amygdala keeps telling you:

Tell yourself:

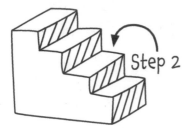

2. Quiet your brain alarm.

This one is a bit trickier because the **fastest** way to quiet your brain alarm turns out to be the **worst** way to do it.

The fastest way to quiet your brain alarm is to take precautions, just in case. To do things like:

→ keep your parents near you all the time

→ take your temperature every day

→ avoid foods you need to chew.

But these aren't the best methods for quieting your brain because they keep your amygdala misfiring, which means it's going to bother you again and again.

FALSE ALARM

TRY TO PROTECT
YOURSELF

BELIEVE IT

So, the better way to quiet your amygdala is to take some deep breaths and tell yourself:

That's just my brain alarm.

I'm okay.

You can also do a mindfulness activity to quiet your brain.

Mindfulness activities help you pay attention to the right thing. Not what might happen, or what could happen, but what is **actually happening**.

There are lots of mindfulness activities. One that's especially helpful is to pay attention to your surroundings.

Breathe deeply and see if you can notice:

Five things you can see.

Four things you can hear.

Three things you can feel (like your feet on the ground or your hair on the back of your neck).

Two things you can smell.

One thing you can taste.

Paying attention to your senses helps your brain to settle down and notice that right here, right now, all is well.

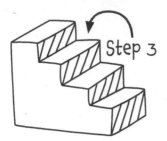

Step 3

3. Stop trying to protect yourself from false alarms.

This is the hardest step, and also the most important.

Pay attention to all the ways you are trying to protect yourself from the health scare your brain is stuck on. Make a plan to eliminate these unnecessary protections, one by one.

→ Go back to eating the foods you used to eat, taking normal-size bites.

→ Practice falling asleep on your own.

→ Challenge yourself to go to the places your family wants to go.

→ Stop taking your temperature, or checking your throat, or asking your parents,

The specific things **you** do might be different from the things you see here. That's okay.

The important thing is to notice what you are doing in response to brain alarms about your health, and purposely move away from those behaviors.

Chances are good that you've been listening to your brain alarm for a while so you might have a bunch of habits you need to undo.

Tackle these habits one at a time.

Your parents can help you figure out how to do this. Or your family can find a therapist, or a book that walks you through the steps for overcoming worries and fears.

There are ideas about additional books you and your parents can read, and websites your parents can visit, at the end of this book.

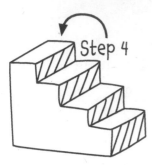

4. Be patient.

It's going to take time and practice to quiet your brain alarm.

Remember the syringe on the kitchen counter? Just like in that example, you are going to notice the scary-seeming thing every day. And in the beginning, you will have to remind yourself, "I don't need to pay attention to that" over and over again.

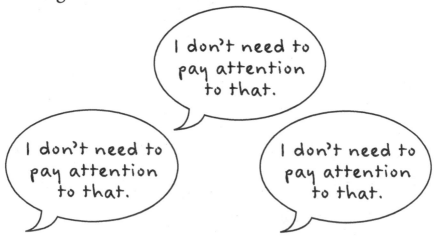

You will probably keep noticing that your stomach feels odd, or it feels scary to chew.

Your brain might tell you—over and over again—that you are going to stop breathing in the night.

And each time, you'll need to tell yourself, "That's my amygdala. It isn't something I need to pay attention to."

FUN FACT
It's normal to pass gas. Lots of it. Most people toot enough in one day to fill a party balloon.

Acting on fears **strengthens them**.

FUN FACT
The smallest muscle in your body is in your ear, a tiny muscle called the stapedius.

Following the steps you just learned
strengthens you.

FUN FACT
The largest muscle in your body is your gluteus maximus, otherwise known as your butt.

You can do it!

You have the knowledge.

You have the courage.

All you need now is the **determination**.

So, what do you think? Are you willing to give it a go?

Just follow the four steps:

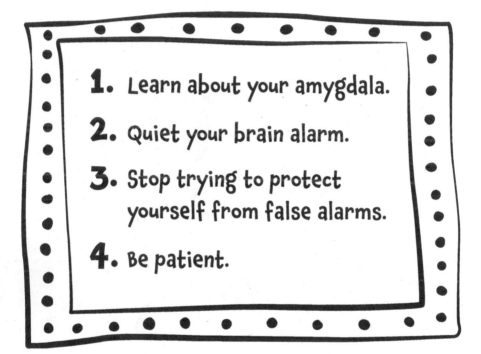

1. Learn about your amygdala.

2. Quiet your brain alarm.

3. Stop trying to protect yourself from false alarms.

4. Be patient.

It might be hard at first, but it's totally worth it.

Because when you follow the steps, your Health Anxiety will get smaller, and smaller, and smaller.

And then you can get on with your life!

Note to Parents and Caregivers

Does your child zero in on every ache and pain?

Are they certain they are going to get a disease, or that their body is going to stop working the way that it should?

Does your child ask for repeated reassurance about their health and wellbeing?

Are they afraid to eat, to sleep, to leave home because they might get sick, get hurt, or die?

If so, your child may have Health Anxiety.

Health Anxiety (often called Hypochondria) is a very real phenomena that affects both adults and children. People with Health Anxiety are excessively concerned about the possibility that something is wrong, or could be wrong, or might go wrong in their body. They panic over seemingly normal body sensations like a gurgling stomach, an achy leg, or a slight headache, and are convinced they are showing signs of diseases they hear about. Children with Health Anxiety plead with their parents to check them, to make sure they are okay.

It's sad for parents to see their children so caught up with their wellbeing, so unable to trust that their bodies are operating as they should. And it can be frustrating, too, because repeated reassurance—and even visits to the doctor—prove only short-term fixes, doing virtually nothing to banish these body-focused fears.

Sometimes children with Health Anxiety do have actual medical issues. Food allergies, for example, or diabetes, or migraines. Children with chronic medical conditions do need to learn how to monitor and live with their conditions, but that's different from fretting and obsessing and endlessly seeking reassurance about their wellbeing.

So, if your child asks you questions about his or her health, stop to think: are they seeking information to help them manage their condition? If so, great. Help your child build their base of knowledge. But be aware that sometimes questions are driven not by a genuine lack of knowledge, but by fear.

Fear-based questions are repetitive. Relentless. Unrealistic.

When your child is asking fear-based (versus fact-seeking) questions, they are often dissatisfied with your answers, and will demand proof that you are right. Children driven by fear do more than what is necessary to try to protect themselves from dangers only they are concerned about.

Parents often try to calm their anxious children by accommodating their fears. They check their children's temperature daily. They show them articles about the signs and symptoms of diseases. They stay right with their child, or serve only the foods their child deems safe, or endlessly reassure, "You're okay. You're okay. You're okay."

Accommodations quiet fear in the moment, but strengthen it in the long run, becoming the glue that cements anxiety in place. Instead of accommodating, parents need to learn to support their children by empathizing with the fear while encouraging a brave response. This book is an excellent starting point for shifting the pattern, helping you and your child recognize the "false alarms" wreaking such havoc in your child's life.

Read this book on your own, first. Then read it with your child in an unhurried way, stopping to talk about the way health fears show up in your child's life.

Pause to enjoy the "fun facts" scattered throughout the book, and marvel together about the wonder of the human body.

Spend time talking about the four action steps at the end of the book. Your child will need your help to practice these steps. Be patient but also persistent. Chances are good that you and your child have patterns set deeply in place so it's going to take time and effort to change things.

If your child is significantly affected by Health Anxiety, you might consider using this book in combination with therapy. And if you struggle with anxiety yourself, you will undoubtedly benefit from the steady presence of a therapist guiding you and your child through this book and additional practice activities. There is a list of resources at the back of this book.

Some additional tips

1. Be aware of your own expression of aches and pains. It isn't necessary to talk about every discomfort you feel, and you certainly don't want to talk—even jokingly—about behaviors you regularly engage in causing heart attacks, or strokes, or cancer.

2. If you are concerned about your child's health, monitor symptoms in a subtle way. Your child is watching you for cues about how serious their situation is.

3. Stay calm in the face of your child's panic, including when they think something is wrong with their body. Remind yourself that your child is scared but not in immediate danger. Empathize with your child, saying things like, "I know. This feels scary to you." Then express faith in their ability to cope, "I know you can get through this." Keep your own breathing steady. Your calm sends a message to the primitive part of your child's brain that is on the lookout for danger. Make sure you are signaling safety.

4. Avoid repeated reassurances. You and your child are likely well versed in a dance in which your child asks, "Am I okay?" (or some version of that question) and you answer, "You're fine; there's nothing wrong!" (or some version of that answer). This needs to stop. Repeated reassurances help your child only for a moment but keep them locked into needing to know with absolute certainty—any time a health concern pops into their head—that the thing they fear is untrue. This reassurance dance keeps children overly focused on the small bumps and bruises and aches and pains and gurgles and arrhythmias that happen in all of our lives.

5. Stop participating in the behaviors linked to your child's anxiety. Your child may insist that you feel their glands, or sleep in their room, or take them to the doctor—and you do those things because you love your child and you see that they are suffering. But these are short-term fixes that keep the problem going in the long run. Acting on anxiety locks worry in place; you need to stop participating in these worry-driven behaviors. Instead, help your child learn to identify "false alarms." Teach your child to calm their brain without capitulating to the fear. Help your

child to have the lived experience of worrying that something is very wrong, and not doing anything about it, and seeing that nothing bad happens.

You can do this. Your child can do this. I'll be rooting for you.

Dr. Dawn

Resources

Organizations

These organizations provide information about childhood anxiety, and include therapist locators to assist with finding specialized care:

USA

The Anxiety and Depression Association of America:
https://adaa.org

The International OCD Foundation:
https://iocdf.org

UK

Anxiety UK:
www.anxietyuk.org.uk

Young Minds:
https://youngminds.org.uk

AU/NZ

Beyond Blue:
www.beyondblue.org.au

Kids Health:
https://kidshealth.org.nz

Please also reach out to your child's pediatrician for names of local providers.

Web-based resources

https://library.jkp.com
Dr. Dawn's Seven-Step Solution for When Worry Takes Over: Easy-to-Implement Strategies for Parents or Carers of Anxious Kids, see page 78.
Video Training Course

www.anxioustoddlers.com
Natasha Daniels of AT Parenting Survival creates podcasts, blog posts, and free resources about anxiety. She also offers subscription courses, coaching, and treatment.

https://childmind.org
This NY Institute offers articles on a host of topics, including anxiety, with a unique "Ask an Expert" feature providing trustworthy, relatable advice.

https://copingskillsforkids.com
Janine Halloran provides free, easy-to-implement, child-friendly tips on calming anxiety, managing stress, and more.

https://gozen.com
Kid-tested, therapist-approved, highly effective animated videos teaching skills related to anxiety, resilience, emotional intelligence, and more.

www.worrywisekids.org
Tamar Chansky of WorryWiseKids provides a treasure-trove of information for parents of anxious children.

Recommended reading

There are many appealing, effective books to help children manage worries and fears. Please check with your preferred bookseller, who can guide you towards books particularly suited to your child's needs. Here are a few suggestions.

For younger children

What to Do When You Worry Too Much: A Kid's Guide to Overcoming Anxiety by Dawn Huebner, PhD, American Psychological Association.

Binnie the Baboon Anxiety and Stress Activity Book by Dr. Karen Treisman, Jessica Kingsley Publishers.

Hey Warrior: A Book for Kids about Anxiety by Karen Young, Little Steps Publishing.

Little Meerkat's Big Panic: A Story About Learning New Ways to Feel Calm by Jane Evans, Jessica Kingsley Publishers.

The Nervous Knight: A Story About Overcoming Worries and Anxiety by Anthony Lloyd Jones, Jessica Kingsley Publishers.

Starving the Anxiety Gremlin for Children Aged 5–9: A CBT Workbook on Anxiety Management by Kate Collins-Donnelly, Jessica Kingsley Publishers.

For older children

Outsmarting Worry: An Older Kid's Guide to Managing Anxiety by Dawn Huebner, PhD, Jessica Kingsley Publishers.

All Birds Have Anxiety by Kathy Hoopmann, Jessica Kingsley Publishers.

The Can-Do Kid's Journal: Discover Your Confidence Superpower! by Sue Atkins, Jessica Kingsley Publishers.

Can I Tell You About Anxiety? A Guide for Friends and Family by Lucy Willetts, Jessica Kingsley Publishers.

Doodle Your Worries Away: A CBT Doodling Workbook for Kids Who Feel Worried or Anxious by Tanja Sharpe, Jessica Kingsley Publishers.

Help! I've Got an Alarm Bell Going Off in My Head! How Panic, Anxiety and Stress Affect Your Body by K.L. Aspden, Jessica Kingsley Publishers.

The Panicosaurus: Managing Anxiety in Children, Including those with Asperger Syndrome by K.L. Al-Ghani, Jessica Kingsley Publishers.

Starving the Anxiety Gremlin: A CBT Workbook on Anxiety Management for Young People Aged 10+ by Kate Collins-Donnelly, Jessica Kingsley Publishers.

For parents

Anxious Kids, Anxious Parents by Dr. Reid Wilson and Lynn Lyons, Health Communications Inc.

The A–Z of Therapeutic Parenting: Strategies and Solutions by Sarah Naish, Jessica Kingsley Publishers.

Breaking Free of Child Anxiety and OCD: A Scientifically Proven Program for Parents by Eli R. Lebowitz, PhD, Oxford University Press.

The No Worries Guide to Raising Your Anxious Child by Karen Lynn Cassiday, Jessica Kingsley Publishers.

Parenting Your Anxious Toddler by Natasha Daniels, Jessica Kingsley Publishers.

Peaceful Parent, Happy Kids by Dr. Laura Markham, TarcherPerigee.

The Yes Brain: How to Cultivate Courage, Curiosity and Resilience in Your Child by Dr. Dan Siegel and Dr. Tina Payne Bryson, Bantam Press.

Dr. Dawn's
SEVEN-STEP SOLUTION FOR WHEN WORRY TAKES OVER

Easy-to-Implement Strategies for Parents or Carers of Anxious Kids

worry has a way of turning into WORRY in the blink of an eye. This upper-case WORRY causes children to fret about unlikely scenarios and shrink away from routine challenges, ultimately holding entire families hostage. But upper-case WORRY is predictable and manageable once you understand its tricks.

This 7-video series will help you recognize WORRY's tricks while teaching a handful of techniques to help you and your child break free.

Each video contains learning objectives and action steps along with need-to-know content presented in a clear, engaging manner by child psychologist and best-selling author, Dr. Dawn Huebner. The videos are available from https://library.jkp.com.

Video One: Trolling for Danger (time 8:15)

- The role of the amygdala in spotting and alerting us to danger
- What happens when the amygdala sets off an alarm
- Real dangers versus false alarms
- Calming the brain (yours and your child's) to get back to thinking

Video Two: The Worry Loop (time 10:15)

- The "loop" that keeps Worry in place
- How to identify where your child is in the Worry Loop

Video Three: Externalizing Anxiety (time 11:41)

- Externalizing anxiety as a powerful first step
- Talking back to Worry
- Teaching your child to talk back to Worry
- Talking back without entering into a debate

Video Four: Calming the Brain and Body (time 13:36)

- Breathing techniques
- Mindfulness techniques
- Distraction techniques
- Which technique (how to choose)?

Video Five: Getting Rid of Safety Behaviors (time 15:18)

- Preparation
- The role of exposure
- Explaining exposure to your child
- Creating an exposure hierarchy

Video Six: Worrying Less Is Not the Goal (time 13:02)

- The more you fight anxiety, the more it holds on
- The more you accommodate anxiety, the more it stays
- Anxiety is an error message, a false alarm
- When you stop letting Worry be in charge, it fades

Video Seven: Putting It All Together (time 19:42)

- A review of the main techniques
- Deciding where to start
- The role of rewards
- Supporting your child, not Worry